Dissolution of Ghosts

For Lea — Thank you for attending. It's great to see you. Best to you with your own great writing.

Dissolution of Ghosts

Berwyn Moore

7/15/05
Erie Book Store

Cherry Grove Collections

Published by Cherry Grove Collections
P.O. Box 541106
Cincinnati, OH 45254-1106

Typeset in Baskerville by WordTech Communications LLC,
Cincinnati, OH

ISBN: 1932339752
LCCN: 2004109693

Poetry Editor: Kevin Walzer
Business Editor: Lori Jareo

Visit us on the web at www.cherry-grove.com

Cover art: "Pomegranates" by Devi Anne Moore (www.tav-art.org)

for Aaron and Emma
and for Brooker,

always

Like love we don't know where or why
Like love we can't compel or fly
Like love we often weep
Like love we seldom keep

W. H. Auden
"Law Like Love"

Grateful acknowledgments are due to the editors of the following journals where some of the enclosed poems first appeared (some in different form):

Birmingham Poetry Review: "Sleep Watch"
Cimarron Review: "The Decisive Moment"
Cottonwood Review: Section 2, "Divorce Dreams" (titled "From a Fourth Floor Window")
George Washington Review: "Measures"
Iris: A Journal About Women: "Pomegranates" (Reprinted by permission)
Journal of the American Medical Association: "Caduceus," "Naming the Days" (Reprinted by permission)
Negative Capability: "What I Want to Tell You"
New Virginia Review: "Boundaries"
New Zoo Poetry Review: Section 7, "Divorce Dreams" (titled "Trying to Leave You")
Phoebe: Journal of Feminist Scholarship Theory and Aesthetics: "Dumbstruck," "River Road" (Reprinted by permission)
The Plaza: A Space for Global Human Relations: "A Story About the Sea"
Poetry Northwest: "A Midsummer Night's Deconstruction of Blame"
Pudding International: The International Journal of Applied Poetry: "Angle of Repose"
River Walk Journal: "Glass," "Skipping Shells,"Section 6, "Divorce Dreams" (titled "Pariah"
Runes: A Review of Poetry: "The Game Lords"
Shenandoah: Sections 1, 4, 5, "Divorce Dreams," "Porch Swing"
The Southern Review: "Exhortation," "Multiple Sclerosis"
Timber Creek Review: "The Bewilderment of Love," "Summer Solstice"
Wild Violet: "Sorghum"
Wisconsin Review: "A Mother's Funeral," "A Woman Carries a Stone to her Grave" (titled "Mountain Night")

Grateful acknowledgments are also due to the editors of the
following anthologies:

Along the Lake: Contemporary Writing from Erie "Dumbstruck,"
    "Multiple Sclerosis," "War Child"
*National Poetry Competition Winners: 1992. Chester H. Jones
    Foundation, Chardon, OH:* "Snake Pit" (4th Place)
Only Morning in Her Shoes: Poems About Old Women. Utah State
    University Press, 1990: Section 8, "Divorce Dreams" (titled
    "Old Woman on the Side of the Road")

Contents

3. Pomegranates

I. Pallor

Pallor

          A pale room with a pale
wooden floor. A woman sits on her bed. Sleepy.
Sleepless. Sweaty sheets crumpled around her.
In the next room, lovers squabble: the shape of frost,
the arrangement of Ursa Major, the mating season
of bears. She thinks about seasons of bearing —
fruit, children, burdens. She touches the lump
in her breast. The lovers croon.

          She sees a rodent, a muskrat
perhaps, at the foot of her bed. She watches as it
pulls itself up on hind feet, staggers toward her,
then folds into a heap. It's dying. She's astonished
that it's so pale, ashen and dusky, and that it
makes no sound. If she could see its eyes or
touch its still chest, she would know who it is.

Glass

I weave a black motorcycle through the shadowy
    tunnels of trees, hunting for crystal stemware

buried in the ground. The engine sputters as I chug up
    a hill, so I leave the woods to get gas. The steel

nozzle enters the tank between my legs; this frightens
    me and I tear away, searching again for the crystal,

my mother's best. When I come to the river's edge,
    I prepare food—spinach balls and chicken heads

stuffed with mint. A boat arrives and an old woman
    picks up the food and leaves me alone on shore

with nothing to eat. I crank the bike, whirling away
    from the woods until I stop again for gas before night

closes in. The attendant inserts the steel nozzle
    in the tank, and in the distance I hear the crystal

shattering, a spray of jagged shards impaling the darkness
    like falling stars. This is someone else's undoing.

I am not lost. I am not hungry. I know where to find her.

Sleep Watch

I enter cautiously, afraid of the specters I know
    are waiting, who every night pull the gauzy brush
        of their gowns against the window. I never
    get used to them. They say nothing, but their glassy
hearts beat in tandem, more articulate than words.

I stand in the room's center, my breathing measured as I
    consider their claim on the room: the unremarkable bed
        with its covers opened to a triangle, preparation I
    made two hours earlier, the desk pressed against the south
wall, its surface cleared of paper, and a slatted chair tucked

beneath it. Light ripples from the lamp to penumbra then
    to total shadow across the floor. I ponder possible
        rearrangement: the bed facing south, or the chairs
    near the window, facing each other. Perhaps then
the specters would leave the room, abandon their hold

by the window, too disturbed by wood scraping across the floor,
    too leery of conversation to find pleasure in staying. Instead,
        I undress, set each item on the chair, and stand naked
    at the edge of the bed, listening to the night contract,
expand and sigh with exhaustion. When I slip into bed,

the weight of darkness settles around my damp skin. I find comfort
    in the mournful cry of a train and the leisurely cadence
        of a man and woman making love over my grave.
I am not afraid to die. My hands curl against my thighs,
and my eyes do not close until morning.

Flashback

A man sat alone in my section.
From the back he looked familiar—the concave
curve of his neck, the

jagged edge of his hairline—but when
he turned around, his gray eyes deflected the light like cheap
ceramic. He told me to

order for him. I brought waffles and coffee,
and when he was done, he demanded both lunch and dinner—
pastrami on rye, cabbage soup, chicken loaf, fried clams, guacamole,
lentils, pickled beets. He ate and ate until

nothing remained. He wrote an address
on an envelope, the letters large and smudged, leaving barely
enough room at the bottom for *San Francisco*. He told me
it was for his daughter on her 13th birthday, but

he was sending it anonymously since a duplicate
of himself was there acting as her father while he hauled his truck
across the country and she didn't know. I asked him why

not send the *other* one out on the road and
he whispered, *because then I couldn't be here,* and he
kissed me so hard

his teeth cut my lips, just like when I
was 13 and he took me to the woods, his eyes glassy
and his breath reeking of glue, and he promised me all
I wanted to eat, then kissed me hard.

Exhortation

My office floats on the ocean—
a cement platform and glass walls
bobbing over foamy swirls. The hulking
oak desk weighs down the north corner,
tilting the floor. In town, people

scurry to leave before a hurricane
blows in. I pack photos and papers,
then see a man I've never seen before
sitting on the stone jetty. I beg him
to come with me, but he refuses.

I return later, kiss him passionately,
and still he sits, wind whipping his hair,
salt encrusting his body in a shroud.
I tell him I love him, but it makes no
difference. At a rescue center, I wander

into a dark kitchen, slimy with seaweed,
and begin snipping the ends off turnips,
a huge pile of them, brown and rotting. I
swear I can hear the man—speaking French
as the waves crash over his head.

Naming the Days

Before dawn when the light tinges
the colorless curtains red or blue,

a factor determined by the cold or lack
of it, but always in summer red, I lie

alone on this bed, my hands hugging
the loose skin of my belly, so suddenly

emptied, and wait for the expected color
each morning to break open the silence,

but it doesn't, and I gasp in the memory
of a moment known again and again

in the frozen quiet of this house. The names
saved up for months I now give to the days,

constant yet pricked and tossed, like
the discarded balloons from a child's first party.

On the Rocky Top
Sierra Nevadas

of a mountain I watch the clouds over
each distant peak assume its shape, billowy
cones nudging the dark edges of ether.
A spider jumps on my knee, its eight legs
orchestrating the thin air until its body drops
to the earth, a tether of fine silk stretching
between us.
           Nothing here holds still,
holds shape long enough to watch or touch
or know its boundaries. You squat beside me,
arched and gnarled like a wind-battered tree,
spitting words hard as granite down the slope.
The spider scuttles to safety under a rock,
the silk between us severed. The clouds
converge with heaviness, unforgiving.

Her Mother's Funeral
for Navana

After three hours of watching others parade
    by her coffin, I was still afraid to look,

convinced they'd used the wrong shade of lipstick
    or dressed her in the ancient tweed suit

she wore to my father's funeral. In the year before
    she died, she called to me as I stomped

from room to room, dusting and scrubbing the house
    she neglected, searching for the mason jars

of gin she hid in cupboards or behind the furnace.
    I couldn't confront her, but I made sure

she heard me breaking the glass jars. She called
    my name from her gloomy room, her voice

as thin and shrill as a cat's, but I outwitted her
    with my silence. Finally, after the visitors had left,

I looked: her skin was not as pale as I remembered it,
    her hands not as frail. I bent over her, eased

my arms under her neck and knees, and lifted her
    wasted body from the coffin. I was the parent,

cradling my wayward child, keeping her from harm,
    singing *hush, hush, it won't be long,* but when I

pressed my lips to her forehead, the shock of cold skin
    pulled me under, the icy currents dragging us both

down. Only my breath rose to the surface:
        Mother, I'm here.

Dumbstruck

On Route 7, I walk through stalled cars
    oddly empty of drivers until I come to a field,
        and there you are! sitting alone on the grass,

clenching your knees with the same hairy hands
    I remember from high school. I haven't seen you
        in years, but you don't have time to chat and point

to a pick-up truck filling with fretful women. No one
    speaks to me on the ride to the city. We stop uptown
        at a windowless trailer where more women

and old men line up to enter. They shiver, perhaps
    from cold. When they emerge from another door,
        some staggering and others crawling, their stunned

faces have been marked with numbers. I run to an alley
    and climb a fire escape. Below me a marching band
        assembles, uncertain of direction until a cop

waves them with a gloved hand toward the trailer.
    Scraggly and off-key, the musicians play a dirge
        as they scuffle through piles of trash, their mournful

notes whimpering behind them, discordant and patchy.
    As I wait for them to pass, I remember the strength
        of your hands as you heaved gravestones—hundreds

of them, engraved with numbers—into the back of a pick-up.
  Easy cash, you said, admonishing me not to tell. And now
    I crouch under the weight of a sky darkening with dread.

Again I'm mute, praying for thunder to crack the silence.

Multiple Sclerosis

When my girls and I arrive at the doctor's office,
I am wearing someone else's shoes, high heels

with tissues stuffed in the toes, and coat,
a too-short sable fur. I leave the coat, shoes

and girls in the waiting room and follow
a doctor who instructs me to climb inside

a massive machine for the first test: interpret
page 72 of Bohr's *Theory of Spectra*, but

the paragraphs seem to float right off the page.
The doctor tells me to sing, but I can't recall

the words to Schumann's "The Wild Horseman."
Try an algebraic equation, he says, but that too

I fail. He takes pictures anyway, and I think
about the tornado years ago, how we huddled

under blankets in the cellar, paralyzed and blind
as we waited for the wind's hideous wail

to weaken with the morning light. We emerged
to a house without a roof, but on the kitchen table,

a birthday cake, its pink frosting swirled into perfect
pink cones, sat untouched. *Whose birthday?*

I wondered. Back in the waiting room my girls
suck candy shaped like radiology probes

and watch cartoons as other women and girls,
decked out in pearls and silky skirts, crowd in.

Before I can pull my girls away from the TV,
the doctor shoos me out, my girls, coat and heels

still inside. I pound on the door, but no one opens it.
Girls, I call. *Don't lock me out. It's my birthday.*

But already, their party is blaring.

The Bewilderment of Love

Elegant people fill this country house
where friends will be married. Someone

has just moved out, bequeathing trash
in the corners and water stains on the ceiling.

No one seems to mind, at least not the bride
who's busy welcoming guests and looking

for her shoes. She assigns me laundry, piles
of sheets and towels, tablecloths, napkins

and frilly doilies to wash and fold while
the others sip pink punch and play croquet

on the plush red carpet. She's right – this
is what I'm good at, I tell myself, then glean

the ravaged tables for a few crushed cream puffs
and follow guests to the river. I toss in a stone

and a man dashes into the murky water, diving
and gasping for air until he pulls out a small girl,

shivering, her lips blue, her pale fist clutching
the stone like a forbidden gift. He wraps her

in a tablecloth, nestles her to sleep in a corner. It's time
for the wedding, but I can't find my shoes.

Measures

This morning's air moves like dark yellow bees,
    thick and sticky with heat. Beyond the porch

screen, small birds shift in a slight tease of wind.
    I am preoccupied with sound and light this mid-

June Sunday as I sit here with you counting out
    sections of orange, measuring spoonfuls

of dark berries into half-cups of delivered cream.
    Always between us it is like this: each day

divided into its parts, privileges I must ask for
    amid moments carefully weighed and packed,

sealed shut against the heat of breath. Nothing ever
    runs over, ever spills out, even by accident.

I watch you now over breakfast and the top edge
    of the *News*, a high sun rising through your hair,

and I swear I could count each unmoving strand. I must
    ask—is it yet that part of day we can speak?

The Chair Wedged Against a Tree

A night wind blasted roof shingles
    through windows, against mirrors,
        into the tub. In the morning, priests

roller skated through the neighborhood, handing out
    escargots and instructions to St. Mary's.
        When I got there, arms heavy with bags

of thawing peas, I found you wrapped in Army blankets
    with another woman, her guide dog growling
        when I spoke, and all you said was *Give me*

a break, it's my birthday. I assured myself I didn't care,
    and turned to join the gray-hairs in a Bingo game,
        careful not to topple buckets of urine along

the way. The old women shouted numbers and gave me bowls
    of spaghetti. I fell asleep eating it and awakened when
        someone scraped a noodle from my face.

Finally, the wind dwindled, and an old man announced I could
    leave. I circled the room with my eyes shut against your
        birthday glee, groping the walls for an exit

and remembered how, years before in a psych lab, I crouched
    inside a dark, soundless vault so long I calculated
        the ratio of systole to exhalation and classified

molecules by color. When they opened the door, the light
    stabbed my eyes, and I knew I should have kept them
        shut. Wind is better than stillness, the way

it repositions the familiar—the chair wedged against a tree, me
here, you there with a woman who can't see your face—
the way it ruffles and tatters what we think is ours.

Divorce Dreams

1.

I fall from a bridge through miles of fog
into cold gauzy water that surges
between my legs and over my head
and under my heart, where at the bottom
mud billows around my feet. Three men
wearing blue suits jump in to save me,
their shoes covered with plastic bags.
They have pockets full of noses, all colors
and shapes, which they arrange before me
on trays like dainty pastries, but I couldn't
care less at the moment for a new nose—
and ask if they have a chair
       or a cup of tea
       or a name
           for the changing color of my skin.

2.

A woman huddles beneath the sill
   of a second story window. She's alone,
frantic to leave, but too afraid to move,
   unaware I can see her. She's neither
young nor old, her face color-worn
   as the walls around her long stripped
of paint. She holds a pink rattle, but the room
   is quiet. I want to tell her about
the white-suited man delivering milk
   to the back door, the two mattresses
flung on the curb, their innards plucked out
   by curious boys, the tailless cat sleeping
under a boxwood. I want to tell her about
   the crawl space in the next room, the one

he doesn't know about, stocked with chips,
    Doctor Barbie, and the keys to his
'57 Chevy. I want to tell her, but I'm huddled
    beneath this window, frantic,
not alone, too afraid to move.

3.
A family outing, you say, so we pile
into the car, kids and dog, a cooler
of pop and baloney, plenty of chips.
You snicker as we arrive at Madame

Demeter's House of Ill-Repute just
across the state line. Two rooms:
a small, dark one with a TV for the kids
to wait in and a large bright one

for orgiastic sex. *Come now*, you plead,
as I gather the children and leave you
there. We drive and drive, devouring
the baloney and chips, telling jokes

and counting green cars, then red ones
until the kids fall asleep and suddenly
we're back where we started at Madame
Demeter's and there you are in her yard,

dazed and grinning, picking up turds.

4.
I fly in a paper plane. Below me,
    houses glitter like tinfoil. An oily river

snakes through fields of old suits
    and shoes planted in rows like corn.

The wind pulls my hair out in single
   strands and drapes them in rows

across the sky. Just when I master the dips
   and dives of flying, someone shoots

at the plane, splintering the wings.
   I wave my white shirt like a flag,

but the bullets whiz and ping and the engine
   fails. My plane falls to the dark river

where I see my shirt burning.

5.
Four kids, none mine, cling
   to the seat and handle bars
      of this old bike with squeaky
         brakes. We fall at the turns, lopsided
            from so many empty cans tied
              to our backs. My legs ache
           and the kids whimper from hunger
        and wet pants. We reach the ocean,
     and a man says I have the wrong ticket.
We scour the dunes for discarded cans.
I'm late for work.
I'm lost.
I can't stop pedaling.

6.
In a burning forest, I jump from stone
   to hot stone as flames singe my hair.

I slip; tangled roots and warm mud

hold me down like a jealous lover.
    I crawl to a metal elevator sliding
        underground and a man waves me in,

barks at me to hurry. But I hesitate—
    afraid of the tight space and darkness.
        A woman in a black dress hands me

unlined paper and a pen to sign my name,
    for permission I think, but the man says
        it's not the *right* paper. I find more,

sign my name again and again, but still
    it's not right and he kicks me out into
        the heat. I run to a cliff where a gondola

glides up the mountain. I yell to the people
    inside, throw stones at the windows,
        but they're playing craps and drinking

champagne and don't hear me. I slog through
    the hot mud, hunting for more paper, watching
        the gondola rise and the elevator sink,

and smelling someone's hair burning.

7.
        I step onto a train wearing
roller skates, a baby strapped to my back,
and roll from car to car looking for a seat.

In one car, veiled women sell smelly seafood—
mussels and inky squids, three tattooed men
hovering over them. In another,
                    I cut through a carpet of wheat
with a pair of scissors and find a child looking
for her mother, and in another, a man displays
his art—photographs of plump women twirling
in an underwater ballet, and still no seat. At
the station, a rabbi leads me to a piano
                where, still standing, I play
Mendelssohn's "Boat Song" until the baby cries,
and the rabbi brings me a chair and finally I sit
and nurse her to sleep. The rabbi hands me a box
from which I pull your dead mother's fur coat,
your latest attempt to lure us back.

8.
We drive by an old woman
on the side of the road

where there's no house,
no barn, no shadowing

husband or trailing child,
no dog, no car parked

on the soft clay shoulder,
no wheelbarrow or basket

for gathering, only the busy
flutter of crows. She's cutting

the roadside grass with a sickle,
bending and swinging her arms

across the berm, a faded print
dress hanging like a whisper

over a body more bone than
flesh, wisps of gray escaping

from a red scarf that blazes
like a halo against the sun.

I tell you to stop the car—I must
join the mystery of this woman's

fierce mission. You let me out,
then speed away, abandoning us

to the heat, the work, the crows
circling above us. I take the sickle,

touch the calluses in the her hands,
then bend and swing, separating

the chaff from the wheat.

9.
A splintery boardwalk on a muddy hill
    leads me to an old trailer where a friend
lies sick. An old man stands sentry and nods
    toward the door where my friend
sleeps under patchwork quilts, then he hands
    me a bowl of melting ice-cream and a spoon.
I eat it down to the dirt at the bottom, then
    I eat that, too, so I don't hurt his feelings.
I tell the old man about my trek here, how I
    climbed rocky hills, tramped through snow,
roamed block after cement block in the city;

how I slept standing against locked gates,
and how I left my husband and a 17-year-old
     prostitute sprawled on a red vinyl sofa
in the library. *It's my job*, she had said.
     My friend rises from her quilts, smiling,
ready for ice-cream, and the old man lifts a baby
     from the window box, brushes off the dirt,
then pats his powdered bottom. The baby laughs
     at the gentle claps, his redemptive voice
floating like balloons around our heads,

     and suddenly we're all laughing —
the old, the lost, the new, the cured.

2. The Decisive Moment

The Decisive Moment

After the photograph, "Suicide,"
by Russell Sorgi, 1942

A woman falls to her death. She is mid-story,
    her right arm reaching toward the sign
that reads: "Genesee Hotel, $1.00 & up, Free Garage."

    She faces the camera, dress fluttering
        around her thighs, legs apart, eyes and mouth
closed in that instant. Below her, a policeman is stepping

                into the building, too late, and patrons
    in the coffee shop are peering out of the window,
unaware,
           as they lunch on ten-cent sandwiches.

     Had loneliness settled so
darkly in her room that she lunged
               for the only light?

And the photographer—
    how long did he take

to focus the lens and set the shutter as she inched her way to the edge?
        How

was he ready for that decisive moment—hers
               and the camera's?

      Yet, it is the camera
that doesn't betray her, that catches her

         mid-fall, so that now I can follow
the curve of her plunge with my finger,

and name her,

        and love her before she hits the ground.

Sons and Daughters

They're at the mall, the Tinseltown
parking lot, playgrounds at dusk. His baggy pants
hang low, his silver Crucifix dangles on a thick chain
around his neck, his hard biceps ripple with coolness.
The gold ring in her navel flickers above her low-rise jeans
as he leans into her. Her hands flutter nervously as he
strokes her thigh. She peeks

over his shoulder checking for an audience,
then licks his ear. She heard today in school that the world
could end, but she doesn't believe it. She thinks of the desert,
the way the dry heat makes her feel small, the way the stars
remind her of eyes. She doesn't know

the sudden twinge in her side is the bursting
through of an egg, its tiny dream-shape holding half
a new world. He squeezes her and she brushes her hand
across his cheek, looks again for someone looking.
She thinks about her mother

curled on the couch, mouth open with sleep,
waiting for her to come home, kiss her on the cheek and climb
into bed. *Hell*—he says,

tugging her to him—*hell, baby,*
we could die together and be okay.

Summer Solstice

Finally, in this west room,
shadows slither in the twilight, tentative shapes
that tease the eye: a wing's flutter, a hand reaching
to pull the lamp string, a ghost waiting to enter,
the illusion of you stepping back into your flesh.

I'm brave at dusk, intermission
between knowing and imagining, between what's
done and what's not. Like your cherry tree,
possessed now by prodigal crows that scatter
the pecked-out fruit across the yard, as though
they know you're gone.

I have waited for this moment
when the hazy tea-colored light of the summer's
longest day embraces your bed, your frayed robe,
your worn daybook, all the things I've yet to touch
since you left.

And then the scrim of darkness
drops and the illusion of movement disappears.
I leave you on the other side, one of us whole
and fed, the other still hungry.

.

Boundaries

Charlottesville, Virginia, 1960

I was six and the steam from curried rice
coiled yellow over my plate and I thought
of our family photos of pale cows idling

in crowded streets, monkeys hanging
on their backs; men chanting and children
watching snakes rise out of baskets;

women clustered together like *pushpa*,
their saris folding in petals around dark
faces, a *tilaka* dotting their foreheads.

I remembered the stories of my mother
with a broken leg that wouldn't heal, me
inside her, and the only doctor, my father,

across another border in Katmandu,
where dancing girls begged him to be
their husband; and stories of his solitary trek

over the boundary of legend where he saw
the yeti, hairy and huge with dangling arms
and hands too human—I thought of this place

where I was born and at that moment when I
was six and eating dinner I knew I would
someday have to return, leave my family here

gathered around a candle-lit table, one
sister dropping crumbs to an over-fed cat,
the other choosing colors for the prom.

I gazed at them over supper, secretly
memorized their faces—my mind
filling like the trunk I would drag—

but their features crossed over like double
and triple exposures: blue-brown eyes, lips
moving without sound, braces, glasses,

pointed nose, crew cut, and blond braid
all on one face—their images would not hold,
would not flatten to sharpness and color.

How would I be ready, not the infant
in a shoe box carried on an elephant,
but the one I would have to become—

alone in two worlds? Now, years later,
the trip never made, that moment
holds as still as any picture, one which I

framed, but in which I do not appear
among the muddle of images, and I try,
again and again, to separate sister from sister,

hand from face, flower from bright fabric,
and legend from the clean, sharp edge
of a table, the border between two histories.

A Story About the Sea

The tide washing over my toes is ghost cold.
A red raft bobs in the water offshore and a man

wearing a black suit and shiny shoes joins me
at the water's edge. Behind us, a wall of lava

begins to roll down the beach, swallowing chairs
and telephone booths, chickens and old tires. I yell

to the man to enter the water and head for the raft,
but he doesn't move, yelling back that he *doesn't*

like cold water. Above us the sky darkens
with the flutter of ravens, but still he doesn't move.

The earth trembles and the hot sand on the beach
falls into itself, swirling down huge, hungry holes.

Still he doesn't come. I leave him on the beach
and head for the raft. The man waves to me,

both arms flapping over his head, flailing wildly
until he loses ground and rises toward the sky,

pushing away clouds of dark feathers with his
frantic flapping until he appears as a pale mist

in the birds' midst, dry-boned and weightless,
an angel with shoes, then disappears like a breath

in cold air. I swim toward the shrinking boat,
now a pinprick of color on the horizon, my legs

throbbing in a tangle of seaweed, my eyes stinging
from the salt, my hands and feet aching with cold.

Sorghum
Buggs Island Lake, North Carolina

The summer we drove to Buggs Island Lake,
my sister and I sat in the back seat, catching

whiffs of honeysuckle and watermelon
while our father played tour guide,

enlightening us on the postcard-perfect
displays of the lives we rolled past:

tobacco fields dotted with bent brown
backs and red kerchiefs, curing barns

where smoke curled from the chimneys
to a flat July sky; crooked shacks hovering

along the roadside, their tin roofs glaring
in the sun, some with weathered porches

and empty rockers, and small yards beaten
smooth as dough where scrawny dogs

slept in the heat; then, the sorghum,
broom-stems as high as the corn

and clustered at the top with dark flowers,
Red Top African, he said, or *Milo Maize*,

their stems thick with sap, ready for pressing.
He stopped the car at a road-side stand,

and three children wearing dull t-shirts
stretched across their chests and britches

the color of hot sand dashed into the picture.
Our father rose from the car, his Panama hat

and sunglasses poised like a movie star's,
took long, even strides toward an old woman

sitting on a crate, and spread open his billfold.
He returned with two quart jars, sticky

and clear-bubbly brown, handed one
to each of us. As he pulled away,

we turned and caught their dark eyes
in ours, held for a moment their questioning,

and we knew, even before tasting it,
that this sweet does not satisfy.

Pigeons

My neighbors hide inside their house,
curtains drawn against August's heat
and the evening's lingering rays that douse

them with unwelcome light. She caresses his feet,
lifts them to the pillow at the end of the bed,
then smoothes and tucks the crumpled sheet

around his swollen middle, kisses his forehead.
The tumor in his belly has defeated him, despite three
rounds of chemo. By Christmas he'll be dead.

For now he sips his meals through a straw she
holds to his lips, her shoulders hunched, her gray
hair a tangle of frizz. He sees her mute tenacity

not as love but as indictment of his body's slow decay
and his mind's dull surrender. I meander
through our yards, pausing in the driveway's

descending dusk to inhale their purple oleander's
lush and fragrant entreaty for death.
And here I grasp, in the faint remainder

of the day, their need for the heavy net
of silence and unbroken shade. I shoo away
the pigeons cooing on their roof, collect

the newspapers from their porch, then wait
for night's fingers to snuff the final ember
from the sky—the darkness, her only escape.

Angle of Repose
San Jacinto Mountains

A skink skitters across a hot rock one instant
    away from my boot, and the fireweed curls
        its petals in the few moments I watch it.

I step carefully across this slope, afraid
    that one stone beneath my weight will disturb
        the rocks from their delicate angle of repose.

Last week in Tijuana, hundreds of chickens
    in an overturned truck smothered in the heat,
        their feathers seized by the wind. Women marked

the spot with a plastic cross and *ocotilla* petals,
    then huddled under serapes, waiting for coins
        from strangers. Tomorrow, I will mail

my daughter chocolates. But tonight, before
    the rocks relinquish their heat and the crickets
        kindle the darkness with song, I will study

angles of slopes with sugar hills on a paper plate.
    I will learn how to gauge the footweight of disturbance.
        I will learn which rock anchors the rest.

Skipping Shells with My Son
Little Bay, Virginia

He taught me the stance: right shoulder bent,
    arm extended, hand parallel to the water

with just the right flick of wrist. He showed me
    that shells, salty and smoothed from the tide,

skip better than stones. The water echoed in rings
    that tugged outward, orbiting around star after flung

star. Swans, watching, skimmed the spray of light,
    then bobbed their ropy necks to catch each fall.

Our feet imprinted our possession of the beach,
    a space between the graceful dip of swans

and the house grounded behind the trees. Gulls
    circled above, hovering for the bread we tossed

skyward. The winter-blue air pecked at our cheeks,
    but we stood firm on our square of sand marked

by the pull of a stick. As we left, he didn't see the tide
    swallow our prints, and for an instant, I thought

I'd never be guilty of betrayal.

Tag

Kate and I run through trees, over hills,
    around houses—we're in a tag race, but I'm not
        sure what we're supposed to tag:

runners or flags or rusted, weedy old cars
    planted like flowers along the path.
        The winners, we learn, get to sing

a song for the judges, accompanied
    by fiddles or a harpsichord, so I'm not sorry
        we come in fifth. We're shoved

onto a stage anyway, along with white gloves and top hats,
    our faces painted white. *It's a mime act,*
        they tell us, *you have two minutes,*

and twenty minutes later, we're still climbing
    invisible ropes and sitting on imaginary chairs.
        The crowd begins to hiss when finally

a little girl wearing beaver skins and mukluks
    leads them in a hearty roundelay. Relieved,
    we leave quickly through a back door,

and Kate weeps as she empties her pockets of twigs
    and broken pencils. *Why didn't you just tell me?*
        I ask, and lead her to the market

where I buy her tuna and canned peas, herbal teas,
    yellow beans, and a giant ham hock.
        At her apartment, I help her

put the food away and find a dead rat
in the cupboard. *Rat-a-tat-tat,*
she says. *There goes another one.*

Pheromones

A cat fish keeps its school together
    with a leader-scent luring every fin
        and gill behind its quivering tail,
    through currents and under swells.
A moth charms her mate with an explosion

of a single molecule, an aromatic spray
    that holds him captive amid a swarm
        of fluttering cousins. Ants follow
    trails of each other single file in a scented
column, then befuddle the weaker ranks who scurry

back in line as slaves. And humans? When you
    lived alone, you didn't bother to shave —
        and discovered later that your beard grew
    twice as fast and your sweat trickled sweeter
when you returned to me. But already, companies

were marketing sweat—bottled, perfumed, ready
    to atomize sensuality. Already, invisible puffs
        tantalized any nose sniffing for company.
    Is this what brought you back, manly man,
or what sent you away again and again?

Snake Pit

Tote-'em-In Zoo
Wilmington, NC

Camera clenched in hand and pencil wedged
    behind my ear, I followed him in—Samson
the Snake Handler wearing enchanted khaki pants
    and a safari helmet, and me, daring reporter,

in summer sandals. Not one stirred as we entered,
    their stillness tangled in shadow, heads, tails,
indistinct. Sleepless eyes guarded every corner —
    rattlers, copperheads, moccasins, orangebrown

crisscrossing their backs, bodies curled into, over
    one another like scraps of flung rope. I focused —
and one by one they awakened, heads charmed
    into motion. They slithered to the beams

overhead and burrowed the crumbling floor, dust
    rising as skin moved ahead of itself. Streaks
of yellow surfaced the heat, cracked through shadows
    as they piled at my feet. I stood dark as timber,

my hands slack, neck tight in a weave of scales
    as I shed my skin, left it heaped on the floor.
My flesh singed cold and dry, my tongue
    split with the absence of words.

Caduceus

for a retired physician

In the evening, I led him through the unattended yard,
guided him with a light touch to his arm over weeds

no longer profound: purple foxglove, yarrow, lobelia,
senna, wild alumroot. *I knew how to use these,*

he told me. *Not many do these days.* After 18 years
away from this place, he remembered the names,

but couldn't distinguish the silvery fuzz on the leaf
of one plant from the lacy white shoot of another;

they were just stalks and sticky weeds invading
the grass, killing it at the roots, like prickly cancers.

All day I waited for him to explain once again
the body's intricate balance of fluids, how it is like

the ocean's perfect balance of water, air, and salt,
and the lungs, alveoli expanding like a prodigal tree,

its claim to each year green and sure-rooted,
and the heart, four-chambered lion he called it,

but instead he said, *do you know the odor of contagion?*
Do you know what it's like to shut the eyes of the dead?

He removed the caduceus from his tie, its winged snakes
dull and tarnished from years of wear, and tossed it

into the weeds. As we turned to go, the still, gray air clotted
with gnats around our heads, hubs of quicksilver consuming the air.

The Game Lords

They are the immortal renewers of substance —
the force behind and above animate nature.

Loren Eiseley, "The Dance of the Frogs"

1. Labrador

Winter, and the Naskapi hide
under Caribou skins and read signs
in the bones of eaten bear. From inside
their tents, they pray to the game lords,
spirits that awaken when the cold breaks
with spring, wet with the songs of frogs.

Their tents shake, their voices unite
with the frog chants, an invocation
for the pounding of hooves, for fish
or fur. They are not silent until morning.

2. Pennsylvania

Lanterns pour their pale light
across a wharf, half-built over
a marsh that swells and sings
with frogs luring their mates.

A lone scientist counts the trills,
measures tones and grunts,
uses his instruments to tap
the mysteries of Naskapi lore.

Curiosity pulls him to the wharf
where his shadow spawns a line of men
alongside him, bounding heel-toe,

heel-toe from one lantern to the next.

He hears the frogs through the mist,
a chorus of trills called by the water.
Their shadows leer up beside him, giants
leaping to the pulse of the night in the wild
wetness of spring, their rhythm driving him
to leap, to keep pace, his shadow changing—
a half-man charging into the cacophony
of the swamp to become one of them—
until the terror that is alone human calls
out to the light on the wharf, shattering
the frenzy into silence.

3. The Explorers Club

A brandy, a cheery fire, chats here
and there of travels and studies,
but he keeps to himself, remembering
that instant between desire and fear,
between the sacred shape of history
and the final leap into darkness,
that instant when knowledge falls
away like cracked teeth.

It is the question of choice, he says,
his batrachian hand hidden in a black glove—
the only proof.

He knows why the Naskapi read
their dreams in bones and wait
for the welcome hush of winter.

3. Pomegranates

A Woman Carries a Stone to Her Grave

This mountain steals the night
        from my body. The blue trees
sway and the milky-eyed moon
        cowers under a cloud. I touch

the stones at my feet, read the names
        with my fingers like Braille.
A man in my room is writing a poem
        about a woman thinking of death.

The moon slides in. Blue trees.
        The moan of a mourning dove.
The woman carries a stone to her grave,
        and the man leads her to a lake

where she sees the faces of her dead
        children in her reflection. She thinks
about the man reconstructing the stories
        of her life, a garden wild with weeds,

aging dogs, and the house she imagines
        that will keep her children safe,
but when she turns to thank him, he is
        a shadow among the trees. The sky

deepens with dawn. I walk to my room
        with a stone, the window open
to the chill, papers fluttering. I let the children
        sleep and collect kindling for the fire.

A Midsummer Night's Deconstruction of Blame

"Lord, what fools these mortals be."
        Shakespeare, *A Midsummer Night's Dream*

At midnight, carpenters renovate my bedroom,
pounding ten-penny nails with a single stroke

while chanting *Jubilate Deo*. You return
from the party with prostitutes, sequined and oily,

who tuck pornographic word games inside
the pages of *Grimm's Fairy Tales* while my parents

sleep downstairs. You beg me to join your frolicking,
but I flee to my sister's room where I find her sleeping

under umbrella palms and maidenhair ferns, peace
lilies and passion flowers. When I wake her up,

she's not surprised at the jungle sprouting around her.
Back in my room, we try to shoo the prostitutes away

when we hear metal clanking outside. From the window,
we see the carpenters spreading metal remnants

from the basement on the lawn—rusted shears,
a broken shovel, two bicycle rims, and a WWII helmet,

the porch light casting shadows behind them
like gremlins. We rush back to my sister's room,

overtaken with ferns and tangled vines, where you

and the prostitutes, quiet now, sit on the floor watching

a spindly spider battle a fist-size wasp, its silvery stinger
unrelenting until the spider weakens with a severed leg.

I glare at you, knowing this chaos is *your* doing,
but as I open the door, the shriveled husk of the wasp

swirls away, its broken wings dissipating like dust,
and the spider begins spinning a new web, her abdomen

pulsating with gold light. The weary prostitutes
collect their games and file out of the house, you

and the carpenters trailing pathetically behind them,
your arms weighed down with useless basement booty.

I hear my parents stirring in their room, the morning
light just petting their door, casting away the night

and the noise, invoking the day's unmarked calm.

...ased when he could take up a straw
...d for the love of God... ."
Conversations with Brother Lawrence

...till

a...   ...reshing floor

dried barle, wheat and rye
grain-straw flattened with hoof

packed tight into burlap, once
beneath swaddling sheets

fiber woven into mats pulling
dirt from our feet or on a

broom end, blunt-cut
for an even sweep, straw

braided strand over strand, baskets
water-tight for babies or church offerings

therapy for heartbroken hands
straw hats and straw-pulp boards

straw cooked for carbon, phenol oil and pitch
straw spun to gold

strawberry, red and sweet
straw worm, straw man

straw house, mud-patched against the wind
straw, smelling of earth and dung

straw worm, straw man, straw
woman with hair the color

of straw, arms and legs stuffed
with straw cut and braided tight

straw woman, spinning each strand to gold
quiet and sure in the night.

Sigh, Pant, Gasp, Wheeze

for Connie H., 1963 - 1974
Babies Hospital, Inc.
Wrightsville Beach, NC

I quit teaching, called instead to hospital
work. I wore a white uniform and bulky white shoes
to Respiratory Therapy, told them what I knew
about IPPB, Mucomyst, and ultrasonic nebulizers.
They sent me to work wiping noses, percussing
chests, adjusting oxygen tubes. In the ward I found
my ex-husband yelling at the kids—Max jumping
on a bed and Connie racing toy wheel chairs across
the floor. I drove my ex to a concert where he hopped
a fence to get in, impatient to join the women in the aisles
dancing and flinging their clothes in the air. I left

        him there, dazed with delight, and returned
to the hospital where laundry lay heaped in the halls,
CAT scanners and defibrillators were tagged
for shipping; even the escalator was defunct. I called
for the kids, for anyone, but the only sound was my own
scratchy voice and the rales and rhonchi rattling
in my lungs. On the street, pallbearers carried
a coffin, Connie's family shuffling behind, though they
were not weeping. I knew I wouldn't either and thought
about our short time together: her crayon pictures of lungs
shaped and colored like upside-down broccoli, her caresses

        on my wrist between masked inhalations
of medicine she said smelled like rotting onions.
I helped her write a letter to the drug company
insisting that *onion* was not a flavor that would cure
her cystic fibrosis, that cherry or grape would better clear
the mucus from her lungs, and that *please if they changed it,*

she would never ever again tease the nurses or throw up
on the floor or complain about the medicine she knew
would save her. But they couldn't, they wrote back,
be a good girl anyway, their letter tucked inside a box
of cherry suckers. And she was. I returned

            to my classroom, called now to the chaos
of chairs, books, humming lights and kids scrambling
before the first bell with reckless energy. I told them
how I had shuffled around the chunks of my life, like pens
and pencils in a box, and what I had learned about the laws
of the heart, systole and diastole, about breath—inhalation
and alveoli expanding. I told them about the sigh, pant, gasp,
and wheeze, words sputtering into coughs, and about desire
and death—how fragile the instant between them. Grief
was a seed we'd plant in a clay pot. They hushed themselves,
and I saw by their imperturbable faces that they wanted nothing.

Porch Swing

The sun sank behind the oak as we pushed
       ourselves against the heat—the chains

over our heads *chinked* front, then *chinked, chinked*
       behind us. We heard the hum of the plane

we'd been waiting for as it skimmed the barley field,
       then rose higher, and headed for the tip of sky

just above our house. No one stirred as the whir
       of speed broke with a sudden thud,

sputtered, then continued, its weakened drone muted
       by the squeak and chink of the swing.

Something dark fell from the sky, dropped to the far
       corner of the field where the children were stacking

treasures in a tower to the sky: shiny metal, laces
       of cable, broken glass, a piece

of rudder, springs, a curved blade, and now, one
       hot, black wheel. They took turns at the top,

hands poised against the backdrop of sun,
       fingers pinching paper wing-tips,

as hazy shifts of wind pushed plane after carefully
       folded plane into the fractured light.

River Road

The old Buick hums as I drive deep
into the Virginia piedmont. Beside me

lies your photograph, taken two weeks
before you died, the sepia tones of your cheeks

dimming like the umber light on these hills.
Your hands, for once still, hang empty.

I stop the car and walk through drizzle
to the water's edge, remembering your hands

that possessed every mirror, sock, and toy
simply because you cleaned them, hands

that yanked the hive right out of its tree,
hands that moved to our faces so fast

we were always caught by surprise.
Two fish ripple the surface, looking

like the shimmering eyes of a dying beast.
A breeze rustles the leaves and I swear

I can feel your hands now, pulling my hair.
But this time, old woman, it doesn't matter.

Your life I wanted, but your death I can
leave behind. I'll head down the river road

with the morning sun on my face,
and the drive will gouge this wound

with distance too complete for your reach.

Field Trip

We climbed aboard an old schooner
docked for tours in the winter lull, mainsail and jibs
rolled and tied to the deck. I played *O Captain,*
My Captain with the kids until a short, red-haired
woman on the bow pulled two bottles from her coat,
pouring from one into the other. *Quiet,* she whispered,
they're bombs, then toddled off

the gangplank and disappeared.
I collected the kids to leave when the boat jerked
from its slip, no one else on board. We found boxes
marked *rigging, halyards,* and *shrouds,* a dead radio,
and a typewriter with a soggy note: *Warn Simon not*
to marry her—she will betray him with her gold chains
and dirty hands. The boat creaked and bobbed.
We grabbed life vests and jumped off,

kicking and sputtering to shallow water.
We trudged to shore, salty and cold, seaweed wrapped
around our heads, and Simon, wearing a baseball cap
and dark glasses, yelled into a megaphone: *Not that way—*
you're supposed to be the heroine! Beside him the short,
red-haired woman, gold chains glittering around her neck,
cleaned her nails and tamped the ashes off a fat cigar.
The dark clouds morphed

to a pasted-on Milky Way, the water
turned blood red as it spiraled down a drain, the ground
rumbled under our feet. I loaded my slingshot with a pebble
and flung it over Simon's head to the trucked-in sand
heaped behind him. *That's a wrap,* he said. The kids and I,
battle-weary and resolute, retreated to our waiting bus, anxious
for its yellow hull to ferry us back to our cluttered desks

and clanking radiator. Gulls circled above, clamoring *victory, victory* into a cloudburst I'm certain was real.

Honey

What I want is simply a night's rest,
    but people lugging family photos
and tarnished candle sticks crowd
    the lobby of this dark hotel. Sadness
saturates the air, and a small girl
    lays her head on my lap. I don't

close my eyes because of the smell.
    A man and woman leave their room
when their child's fever cools.
    The girl and I rush in, but no one
comes to clean it. A man pokes
    his waxy head in the door to say

he's ready for the girl. He doesn't
    smile, and I realize this isn't a hotel—
it's a hospital. An orderly wheels
    the girl away, and a nurse escorts
me to the kitchen where I'm told
    to sauté chicken and bean sprouts.

When someone tosses a raw frog
    into the skillet, I am so afraid
of the germs, I burn everything.
    I find the girl in the dining hall,
and we join a dark-skinned family
    arranging tarnished candle sticks

    on a long table. I offer my chair
and the charred food to the oldest
    woman who offers me honey. She
lifts her hands to my lips and says,

Out of the eater, something to eat,
out of the strong, something sweet,

and I taste how sweet it all becomes,
    how the stickiness embraces us
in a sweet delusion, how inconsequential
    our flaws and fears seem as they melt
into clover, orange, tupelo, alfalfa,
    how easy it is to fall asleep.

Keys

True love is tongueless like a crocodile.
Robert Herrick's "To Mistress Ann Potter"

The baby slept while I drove to the spot
    marked X on my scribbled map, a house
        perched on stilts over a salt marsh.

Tuxedoed men and glittery women meandered
    through dingy rooms, sipping champagne
        from paper cups. You were laughing

and flirting with a covey of women and pretended
    not to know me. I decided to leave, but couldn't
        find my coat or keys. Little girls in petticoats

led me to a room where we waited in line to play
    a ramshackle piano. When it was my turn,
        the keys *plinked plinked* with dullness,

the baby cried, and the tuxedoes and glitter slunk
    out of the room. I collected all the dirty spoons
        and plates, but still you didn't acknowledge

me. One by one your women fluttered away,
    and when I pretended not to notice, you
        brooded like a peacock with a tattered tail.

A boy ran toward me wearing my coat.
    He pouted when I asked him for my keys.
        On the porch, I held his hand while crocodiles

scuttled under the floor boards. We left together—
    the boy, the baby and I—unruffled by the absence
        of speech or the swish of crocodile tails.

We left you plinking the keys of the old piano,
    an afterthought in the darkness, with no one
      there to tell you it wasn't your turn.

Winter Feast

Blessed are those who are invited
to the wedding supper of the Lamb.
Revelation 19: 9

I had just begun to clean the stairs,
    kneeling at the bottom with a brush

and sudsy water, when you barged through
    the door. You were not yourself,

but a duplicate, a hollowed-out core of waxy skin
    cracking from the cold outside. I left

the brush on the third step as you pulled me up
    and dragged me to the hospital where

through isolation room windows we saw you
    lying pale and still on a gurney, tubes

and monitors attached to your bare chest. But
    it was too late—there was nothing they

could do to bring you back, so I left you there
    watching yourself die and returned

to my stairs and sudsy water. By dark the guests
    had arrived, anxious for the feast. I took

my assigned seat next to yours, empty of you
    and the self you concocted to cheat me

of the place I didn't know was mine until now.
    As the host lifted his glass, I heard you

outside, drunk and laughing, oblivious to the cold,
malignant air even as it consumed you.

Sanctuary

The baby nestled in my arms wasn't mine.
You didn't want to see me, so I took him

home and watched a movie with no sex in it
just to spite you. When the baby woke,

I pushed his stroller through wet sand toward
the south end of the beach to a cottage

where we hid from two men in dark suits
and white gloves. I packed food into damp

paper bags and from the window I saw the men
carrying a naked man with sandy hair—it might

have been you—to the ocean. One held his feet
and the other his hands as they swung him

like a hammock and tossed him into the waves.
We rushed out and headed north on a beach

crowded with sunbathers and kids digging holes.
A dog sniffed at the baby, then trotted away.

I saw you lying on a blanket, your eyes closed
and skin puffy and pale, but I pushed on.

At dusk, we came to a stone house with no windows,
only a quaint door from which an old nun waved us

frantically inside. *Let us not die, and not rush
into the heart of the fight,* she said. And there,

in the darkness—with the damp smell of ripening fruit
and the rustling of a long frock, her purgatorial fingers

brushed my cheek, and the night unraveled like a lullaby.

War Child

Put new wine into fresh skins;
then both are preserved. Matthew 9:17

Magda, my dark-eyed daughter, you have found me
    in this dream. At seven, you are older than I expected,
        and quiet, your English tumbling out in one-syllable

questions: *home? far? food?* We sit in a caseworker's
    cluttered office as she hands me form after form
        to sign and explains your missing toes—frostbite

(a broken boiler at the orphanage), your missing surname
    (no birth record), and your missing twin (land mine).
        She leads us through a maze of musty rooms

inhabited with the spectral relics of other children—
    their sorrows and rotten shoes, an empty cup,
        the taste of blood—all shed here like snake skins

turned inside out, withered, impotent. Each room
    becomes successively darker and smaller until
        we enter a bright nursery where a few other locals

hold the hands of dark-eyed children. The caseworker
    invites us to pick figs from branches that reach
        through the window, and a small boy plays

on a violin the quick, trill notes of a gypsy rondo.
    A Siamese cat curls around a brood of peeping
        chicks. You name it Kasyan, after your sister.

The woman gives each new family a test; for us,
    in small backward letters we hold up to a mirror,
        she has written *peanut butter.* So we create

a cake, gooey and sweet, guessing the shakes of cinnamon
and the measure of milk. When you lick the spoon —
first timidly, then like a bear—another remnant

of war falls from your shoulders. We pass around
the spoon. The others applaud. It's time to go home.

What I Want to Tell You
for Brooker

Nowhere, beloved, can world exist but within. Life passes in transformation. And, ever diminishing, vanishes what's outside.—Rilke

1.
After that ride on the Harley,
I huddled in the silent hole of myself,
renouncing my name, feeling only
the black clot of a night kept hard
and secret. There were no shoots
growing from a soft green center,
only a dark, hard knot from which
nothing grew.

      I saw him at school,
in stores, my teacher's office, beside me
at the movies, posed cleverly against
the tree in our yard. His face was always
at a window. He was the man down
the street skimming the evening news,
who told his daughter to change her
blouse before going out the door.

2.
I found salvation in silence: nothing
had been lost and death was just

a word or a lie, detached from grief
and fear. The first time your hand

touched mine I wanted to tell you,
this is not me, there's another—

a forgotten one, but you didn't pull
back your hand and its touch was like

the bristly embrace of a summer storm
and here I am—unafraid, light hovering

over our bed like a sheet of moons. Now,
when I hear the sound of my voice, I know

the story it tells is not past or present,
not death or absence; it is *our* voice, our tale,

and its telling is like the instant between
seasons, necessary and brief. I want to tell you

how it is when you touch the center, how
the hard knot opens like a lily, how easy

it is to let the weight of you fall over me
and into me, no heavier than the light falling

around us, how our flesh forgets its boundaries,
how you hold my name in the sure curve

of your voice, and how, finally, we achieve
it: the dissolution of ghosts.

Pomegranates

In a crowded doctor's office, nurses
admonish a woman, pale, sweaty, and hungry
    from the wait, to be patient. All the chairs
are filled, so she shuffles to the corner to sit
    on the floor. A rodent, a muskrat she thinks,
jumps out from under a table, spewing a thick,
    white liquid from its mouth. The woman grabs
the waiting children and rushes them to the pier
    where they board a ferry. The captain speaks
a language the woman doesn't recognize,

        but he's kind. She sits with a prostitute
who leads the passengers in charades and peels
    pomegranates for the children, letting them spit
the ruby seeds in her dark hands after sucking the sweet-
    tart pulp. The boat docks at a red cottage, tiny
from the outside, but inside, sunny with lush fountains,
    stacks of books, the scent of almonds. The prostitute
hums in the spangled air, her voice a wild invention of clang
    and comfort as she and the woman sit. The nurse calls
for the woman, but the lump in her breast has disappeared.

Notes

"The Decisive Moment":

>Henri Cartier-Bresson, photographer, coined the term "decisive moment": *If the shutter was released at the decisive moment, you have instinctively fixed a geometric pattern without which the photograph would have been both formless and lifeless.*

"A Midsummer Night's Deconstruction of Blame":

>Mechanical problems in WWII military aircraft were sometimes blamed on gremlins.

"The Calling":

>IPPB is intermittent positive pressure breathing.

"Honey":

>*Out of the eater, something to eat; out of the strong, something sweet*: Samson's riddle (Judges 14:14).

"War Child":

>Galina Samoilova reported that his male Siamese cat, Kasyan, slept with and protected a brood of baby chickens at his home near Novichikha, Russia (*Itar-Tass*).

"Sanctuary":

>Adapted from Virgil: *Let us die, and rush into the heart of the fight.*

Berwyn Moore was born in Mussoorie, India, and grew up in Colorado, Michigan and Virginia. Her poetry has been published in *The Southern Review*, *Shenandoah*, the *Journal of the American Medical Association*, *Kansas Quarterly* and other journals. She has won poetry awards from the Chester H. Jones Foundation and Negative Capability press and a teaching award from the National Foundation for the Advancement of the Arts. Her poem "Glass" was nominated for the Pushcart Prize. Before studying English at the University of North Carolina and Bowling Green State University, where she won the Devine Fellowship Award, she worked as a photographer, a hospital pharmacy IV technician, and a respiratory therapist at a children's hospital. She is an Associate Professor of English at Gannon University in Erie, Pennsylvania, where she lives with her husband, Robert Brooker. She has two children, Aaron and Emma, and two stepchildren, Rachel and Ian.

Printed in the United States
31546LVS00005B/331-339

9 781932 339758